Date	#	Description			

Date	#	Description	In	Out	Balance

Date	#	Description	In	Out	Balance

Date	#	Description	In	Out	Balance

Date	#	Description	In	Out	Balance

Date	#	Description	In	Out	Balance

Date	#	Description	In	Out	Balance

Date	#	Description	In	Out	Balance

Date	#	Description	In	Out	Balance

Date	#	Description	In	Out	Balance

Date	#	Description	In	Out	Balance

Date	#	Description	In	Out	Balance

Date	#	Description	In	Out	Balance

Date	#	Description	In	Out	Balance

Date	#	Description	In	Out	Balance

Date	#	Description	In	Out	Balance

Date	#	Description	In	Out	Balance

Date	#	Description	In	Out	Balance

Date	#	Description	In	Out	Balance

Date	#	Description	In	Out	Balance

Date	#	Description	In	Out	Balance

Date	#	Description	In	Out	Balance

Date	#	Description	In	Out	Balance

Date	#	Description	In	Out	Balance

Date	#	Description	In	Out	Balance

Date	#	Description	In	Out	Balance

Date	#	Description	In	Out	Balance

Date	#	Description	In	Out	Balance

Date	#	Description	In	Out	Balance

Date	#	Description	In	Out	Balance

Date	#	Description	In	Out	Balance

Date	#	Description	In	Out	Balance

Date	#	Description	In	Out	Balance

Date	#	Description	In	Out	Balance

Date	#	Description	In	Out	Balance

Date	#	Description	In	Out	Balance

Date	#	Description	In	Out	Balance

Date	#	Description	In	Out	Balance

Date	#	Description	In	Out	Balance

Date	#	Description	In	Out	Balance

Date	#	Description	In	Out	Balance

Date	#	Description	In	Out	Balance

Date	#	Description	In	Out	Balance

Date	#	Description	In	Out	Balance

Date	#	Description	In	Out	Balance

Date	#	Description	In	Out	Balance

Date	#	Description	In	Out	Balance

Date	#	Description	In	Out	Balance

Date	#	Description	In	Out	Balance

Date	#	Description	In	Out	Balance

Date	#	Description	In	Out	Balance

Date	#	Description	In	Out	Balance

Date	#	Description	In	Out	Balance

Date	#	Description	In	Out	Balance

Date	#	Description	In	Out	Balance

Date	#	Description	In	Out	Balance

Date	#	Description	In	Out	Balance

Date	#	Description	In	Out	Balance

Date	#	Description	In	Out	Balance

Date	#	Description	In	Out	Balance

Date	#	Description	In	Out	Balance

Date	#	Description	In	Out	Balance

Date	#	Description	In	Out	Balance

Date	#	Description	In	Out	Balance

Date	#	Description	In	Out	Balance

Date	#	Description	In	Out	Balance

Date	#	Description	In	Out	Balance

Date	#	Description	In	Out	Balance

Date	#	Description	In	Out	Balance

Date	#	Description	In	Out	Balance

Date	#	Description	In	Out	Balance

Date	#	Description	In	Out	Balance

Date	#	Description	In	Out	Balance

Date	#	Description	In	Out	Balance

Date	#	Description	In	Out	Balance

Date	#	Description	In	Out	Balance

Date	#	Description	In	Out	Balance

Date	#	Description	In	Out	Balance

Date	#	Description	In	Out	Balance

Date	#	Description	In	Out	Balance

Date	#	Description	In	Out	Balance

Date	#	Description	In	Out	Balance

Date	#	Description	In	Out	Balance

Date	#	Description	In	Out	Balance

Date	#	Description	In	Out	Balance

Date	#	Description	In	Out	Balance

Date	#	Description	In	Out	Balance

Date	#	Description	In	Out	Balance

Date	#	Description	In	Out	Balance

Date	#	Description	In	Out	Balance

Date	#	Description	In	Out	Balance

Date	#	Description	In	Out	Balance

Date	#	Description	In	Out	Balance

Date	#	Description	In	Out	Balance

Date	#	Description	In	Out	Balance

Date	#	Description	In	Out	Balance

Date	#	Description	In	Out	Balance

Date	#	Description	In	Out	Balance

Date	#	Description	In	Out	Balance

Date	#	Description	In	Out	Balance

Printed in Great Britain
by Amazon